BANANAS DON'T GROW ON TREES

A GUIDE TO POPULAR MISCONCEPTIONS

Joseph Rosenbloom
Illustrations by Joyce Behr

 STERLING PUBLISHING CO., INC.   NEW YORK

 Oak Tree Press Co., Ltd.
London & Sydney

OTHER BOOKS BY THE SAME AUTHOR

Biggest Riddle Book in the World

Daffy Dictionary

Doctor Knock-Knock's Official
Knock-Knock Dictionary

Gigantic Joke Book

*Dedicated
to "Big" Al Backerman with love*

Second Printing, 1979
Copyright © 1978 by Joseph ROSENBLOOM
Published by Sterling Publishing Co., Inc.
Two Park Avenue, New York, N.Y. 10016
Distributed in Australia by Oak Tree Press Co., Ltd.,
P.O. Box J34, Brickfield Hill, Sydney 2000, N.S.W.
Distributed in the United Kingdom
by Ward Lock Ltd., 116 Baker Street, London W.1
Manufactured in the United States of America
All rights reserved
Library of Congress Catalog Card No.: 78-57783
Sterling ISBN 0-8069-3100-0 Trade   Oak Tree 7061-2594-0
3101-9 Library

Contents

plants

"Bananas don't grow on trees!"

Bananas grow on trees

If by a tree one means a plant with a woody trunk that survives from one season to the next, then there is no such thing as a banana tree. The banana fruit actually grows on a stalk. While the banana plant may reach a height of 30 feet (9.1 m), and resembles a tree in size and shape, it does not have a woody trunk. The stalk consists of the lower ends of the leaves, which overlap and are tightly bound together.

The banana plant bears fruit for only a single season. Then the portion above ground dies, leaving an underground stem which grows into a new banana plant the following season.

The peanut is a nut

The peanut is not a nut. Most nuts grow on trees. The peanut plant is a legume, a member of the pea family, and the peanuts it produces grow underground.

Trees receive most of their nutrition through their roots

Not so. Roots are necessary to the tree because they anchor it, and because they take up moisture and minerals from the soil. However, the leaves play an even more important role in the nutrition of the tree. Leaves, using chlorophyll (the substance which makes them green), are able to convert carbon dioxide and water into food in the presence of sunlight. This process is called photosynthesis. It is in the leaves, not in the roots, that the manufacture of food for the entire tree goes on.

Every tree has only one kind of leaf

Not the sassafras tree. This tree, a common North American member of the laurel family, has leaves of three distinctly different shapes. One kind of leaf is basically oval and unlobed, another is shaped like a mitten with a thumb on one side, and the third is three-lobed with "thumbs" on both sides. All three of these leaves may be found on the same tree, and even on the same twig at the same time.

The leaves of mulberry trees also have various shapes.

A tree grows by lengthening its entire trunk

Most people, if asked, would assume that a tree grows pretty much like other living things — that the trunk merely stretches upwards as the tree grows. This is not really what happens.

Actually, a tree grows in height as a result of cell division and enlargement that occurs only at the *top* of the trunk. Thus, a tree gains height through the growth of new wood at its uppermost region. A tree gains thickness because cells in the outer layer of the trunk also divide and increase in number, adding new layers. So, a tree can be said to grow as a result of the gradual accumulation of wood, layer upon layer, extending up the outside of the trunk and over the top. This growth pattern is the reason why the branches of a tree do not rise higher above the ground as the tree grows taller, and explains why two nails driven into a tree trunk close together do not drift apart over the years as the tree increases in circumference.

The branches and twigs of the tree grow in the same way.

Redwoods are the oldest trees

The huge redwood trees of California (also called sequoias) grow to be very old — several thousand years old, in fact — but they are not the oldest trees. "General Sherman," the name given to a giant sequoia in Sequoia National Park in California, is the largest living thing in the world: 272 feet (83 m) high and 37 feet (11 m) in diameter at the thickest part of its trunk. However, it has been around a mere 3,500 years.

A far less spectacular tree in height and width, the bristlecone pine, often reaches this age and even exceeds it. This tree is usually found at elevations above 10,000 feet (3,048 m) in the American West, and a specimen 4,000 years old is not uncommon. The oldest known specimen, 4,600 years old and aptly named "Methuselah," was found in the White Mountains in California. The potential life span of a bristlecone pine is estimated to be 6,000 years. The giant redwoods are babies by comparison.

Forest fires are harmful to all trees

Some trees, surprisingly, need forest fires to survive. The cones of the jack pine open and release seeds only after exposure to intense heat. In this way nature insures that the jack pine will grow again after a forest fire.

The century plant

The century plant blossoms every hundred years

The century plant got its name under false pretenses, because of the mistaken notion that it blossoms only when it reaches 100 years. The fact is that no century plant even survives such a period of time.

How long it takes the plant to blossom depends on the plant and on the conditions under which it is growing. In warmer climates, the plants may blossom every 5 to 10 years. In cooler climates, especially the United States, the plants generally take longer to blossom, sometimes as much as 20 or 30 years. The plant may grow 60 years or so, at most, before it blossoms.

The willful weed

A weed is a species of plant

A weed is merely an unwanted plant. Therefore, there are no species of weeds because a plant may be a weed in one place but not in another. The morning glory in the home garden is an ornamental plant; in a soy bean field, it is a weed. A corn plant growing in a wheat field would be a weed — and vice versa. Many other plants are similar: they have value in one situation and are pests — that is, weeds — under other conditions.

animals

**Keeping track
of animal gaits**

All four-legged animals move their legs in the same order

Not true. Four-legged animals move forward in two different ways. The most common pattern is the diagonal motion of the trot, in which the right front leg and the left rear leg move forward in unison, followed by a similar movement of the left front leg and right rear leg. The other gait is the pace, in which the legs on the same side of the body move simultaneously in a lateral pattern: right front leg and right rear leg, then left front leg and left rear leg.

Most four-legged animals are trotters, but some, like the giraffe and the camel, are pacers. Harness racing, of course, features horses with both gaits, but pacing horses are trained to this unnatural gait with hobbles.

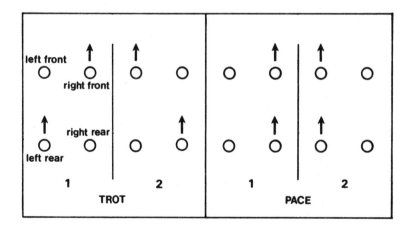

All animals lie down to sleep

Humans may have to lie down to sleep well, but many animals do not. The horse, for one, sleeps far better standing up than lying down. Horses have been known to go for months on end without lying down. However, both horses and cattle, especially when in herds, may lie down, one at a time, with legs outstretched and sleep deeply for several minutes.

The horse can relax and sleep while standing up because its leg joints automatically lock in place to support the animal. It is as if the animal were standing on stilts.

Elephants, zebras, antelopes and many other plant-eating animals are also able to sleep on their feet.

All animals crave salt

No. All animals lose a certain amount of salt each day, and must replace it to remain healthy. However, some diets provide more salt than others. Animals which feed exclusively on plants (cattle, horses, antelopes, and so on) crave salt because they do not get enough from their normal diet. Carnivorous (meat-eating) and omnivorous (meat- and plant-eating) animals (including man), on the other hand, have no such need to supplement their diets with salt; they get all the salt they need from the blood and flesh of the animals they eat.

The rabbit's rear-view vision

No animal can see behind its back while facing forward

Hunters who have approached rabbits from behind only to have them scurry off know this is not so. Because a rabbit's eyes are set on the side of its head and protrude somewhat, it can virtually see in a full circle (as well as upwards) even when its head remains motionless.

Antelope, deer and other animals that need to be alert to avoid being killed by predators also have this kind of vision.

The eyes of some animals shine in the dark

No animal has eyes that actually shine. The glow we see in the dark is caused by reflection alone. The proof? Animals' eyes do not shine in total darkness, but only if one shines a light into them.

What causes the eyes of many animals to glow in darkness, often in bright red, yellow and green colors, while human eyes rarely throw back even a glint when light is shined into them in the dark? It seems many animals have a structure in each eye known as the tapetum, which reflects whatever light enters the eye. Once in a while a tapetum is present in the eyes of a human, who may be thought to possess some mysterious super-human power because of his or her blazing eyes. This is nonsense, of course. All it means is that the eyes of this person can reflect light — no more.

The size of a newborn animal depends on the size of its parents

Not necessarily. The size and condition of an animal at birth often depend more on where it is born and the circumstances of its infancy than on the size it will be when it reaches adulthood. The newborn of many species of deer and antelope are large in relation to the size of their parents, and quite strong, able to stand and walk shakily very soon after coming into the world. Why? These animals are in many cases required to move with the herd almost immediately after birth. They must rely on speed to avoid being caught and killed by other animals, which often seek out the young when attacking a herd.

Black bears of North America, on the other hand, are quite small at birth. Adults usually weigh between 200 and 300 pounds (91 and 136 kg), and individuals weighing 600 pounds (272 kg) have been reported. The bear cub, however, is born blind, toothless, hairless and helpless in a den in the middle of winter, weighs only 8 ounces (.23 kg) and is about 8 inches (20.3 cm) long. The bear can afford to begin life so weak and helpless because it is cared for by its mother for at least the first year of its life. Unlike the young deer and antelope, it does not have to face problems immediately after birth.

The newborn of many marsupials (animals having pouches in which the young are carried) are also far smaller than one might expect. A kangaroo is about an inch (2.5 cm) long when born; an opossum at birth is about the size of a bumblebee and weighs 1/15 of an ounce (1.9 g).

Animal litters are always a mixture of male and female

While it is generally true that animal litters contain members of both sexes, there is at least one exception. The nine-banded armadillo gives birth to four babies of one sex at a time — always either all male or all female. Are the numbers of male and female born equal in all animals? Again, this is generally so, but with an interesting exception. Among greyhound dogs, more males are born than females. For every 100 female greyhounds, 110 males are born.

If an earthworm is cut through in the middle, both halves will grow into new worms

This is not true, although the earthworm does have the ability to regrow some parts.

If the last five of the earthworm's 115 to 200 segments are cut through, it will grow new ones rather quickly. Even if more than this is cut off, the worm will probably grow a new tail, although usually the process of regrowth is delayed and only four or five segments are restored.

However, if the worm is cut in the middle, this is too serious an injury for recovery of *both* halves. The front half may regrow a shortened tail and become a whole (but shorter) worm again. The rear half, however, would not be able to grow a new head. Earthworms have sometimes grown new head regions after up to 15 segments were cut off the front end, but in the case of an individual severed in the middle, between 60 and 100 segments would be cut off — far too many to allow regrowth of the head. Thus the rear half of a center-cut earthworm dies or, occasionally, grows a new tail at the cut end, in which case the resulting worm with a tail at both ends dies of starvation.

Other kinds of worms have even more remarkable powers of regrowth.

The earthworm makes a comeback

**Some just
will not drink**

All animals drink

No. All animals need water, but not all animals get their water by drinking. The kangaroo rat, an inhabitant of desert regions in the southwestern United States, is able to get along without drinking water, getting its moisture from the plants it eats. Other animals very seldom drink water. Giraffes can go for weeks without drinking. They, too, manage to get enough moisture from the foliage they feed on. Most sheep and gazelles drink infrequently. A few lizards are able to meet their water needs largely by absorbing it through their pores.

Mammals

The whale spouts water

When a whale "blows," it looks as if it is spouting water but it is really blowing out air.

Before a whale dives, it fills its huge lungs with air, and it can hold its breath for as long as an hour before it surfaces. When the whale comes up to the surface again, it blows out the air in a great blast through one or two nostrils, called blowholes, on top of its head. When this air, which has become warm and moist in the whale's lungs, meets the colder air of the atmosphere, it condenses into a steamy vapor. The colder the air around the whale, the more visible the vapor when the whale exhales. Much the same thing happens to humans on a cold day, when we can "see our breath" as we exhale.

Thus, the whale does not spout water. A true mammal, it can no more tolerate water in its breathing system than we can.

The elephant drinks with its trunk

The elephant does not take water in through its trunk. It drinks with its mouth just as we do, but first it sucks water into its trunk. It then inserts its trunk into its mouth, lets the water out there, and swallows it.

How do baby elephants nurse? The trunk is pushed aside during suckling and the baby elephant uses its mouth to obtain nourishment, as do all mammals.

Elephants are afraid of mice

This is a common belief that has been around a long time, but there is not the slightest particle of truth to it. Mice often infest the cages of elephants in zoos and circuses, but no keeper has ever reported any elephant even mildly upset by the little animals. Usually, the mice scurrying after food on the floor of the cage are simply ignored by the elephants.

The elephant is the longest-lived mammal

Actually, from all available evidence no mammal exceeds man in length of life. While stories of extreme old age among humans are often exaggerated (some older persons tend to "add" a few years), there are many authenticated cases of persons reaching well over 100 years. The greatest verified human age has been reported to be 113 years.

What about elephants? The oldest recorded age is only 70 years. Even the whale is believed to live longer, although little is definitely known about the longevity of whales.

The hippopotamus sweats blood

The skin of the hippopotamus does secrete a thick, oily, reddish substance that gathers in droplets on the skin. This secretion helps to prevent the animal's thick hide from drying and cracking, especially when the hippo is out of water. The protective fluid flows more freely and becomes a darker red when the animal is hot, excited or in pain. However, although it resembles blood in color and texture, the fluid is not blood and has no blood in it.

The lion is the king of beasts

The male lion is such a handsome, majestic-looking creature that it is little wonder he has become the symbol of royalty. But his appearance is deceptive. His behavior is far from kingly, or even gentlemanly.

1) The lion is not the strongest creature in his domain. If a lion met an elephant or a rhinoceros on a narrow path, he would be the first to move over. The lion is not even the largest of the cats; the Siberian tiger (unfortunately now almost extinct) is larger and stronger.

2) Lions fail to kill their prey quickly more often than cheetahs and leopards, which nearly always make quick, "clean" kills. Particularly when an older lion or a lioness hunts alone, without the aid of the rest of its family (called a pride), its first strike often does not bring down the zebra or large antelope, and it may be minutes before the suffering animal is killed.

3) The female does 90 per cent of the killing, but the male then shoves her aside and feeds first. Only after he has satisfied his hunger does he permit the lioness and the rest of the pride to feed.

4) Both male and female lions sometimes eat their own cubs.

5) The lion is sometimes as much a scavenger as a regal hunter. In some instances, lions get as much as half their food from carcasses killed by hyenas, wild dogs or disease.

Although he may not be king, the lion is a good survivor and not an endangered species.

The king of beasts?

The lion is a creature of the jungle

A popular notion is that lions inhabit the jungle. Nothing could be further from the truth. The lion is an animal of the open bush, great grassy plains and semi-desert regions that cover much of Africa.

Lions are found only in Africa

The lion once ranged over Eastern Europe, the Middle East and western Asia as well as Africa. Lions became extinct in Greece in ancient times, and in Europe and the Middle East by the end of the first century A.D.

Modern lions are not native to Africa alone. Some lions are still found in India, where they are now confined to the Gir region, a semi-desert and scrubland area on the Kathiawar peninsula.

The hyena is a coward and a scavenger

The hyena is not entirely cowardly, nor is it only a scavenger. Although it feeds primarily on dead animals, it is also an active and aggressive hunter, feared by many (even larger) animals for its ferocity. They usually hunt in packs, but a single hyena can bring down a full-grown zebra. The hyena's jaws are among the most powerful in the animal world.

The backslapping bear

Bears hug people to death

An unarmed person attacked by a bear is in great danger, but will he be hugged to death? The "crushing embrace" or "deadly hug" of the bear is just a legend.

Bears injure and kill their victims with a mighty wallop of their forepaw. They also use their powerful teeth and their sharp claws. There is not a single instance on record of a person being hugged to death by a bear.

Bears hibernate in winter

Some animals retire to underground shelters to pass the winter months when the weather is cold and food is scarce. The life processes are slowed down to the barest minimum to conserve energy and yet sustain life. When the woodchuck hibernates, for example, its body temperature drops drastically and its heart slows down to a pace of much fewer beats per minute. Hibernating animals are deeply unconscious.

What about bears? In spite of the commonly held view, bears are not true hibernators. Rather, they sleep during the long winter months. None of their vital functions are significantly reduced. They can easily be awakened from their "hibernation" and will become fully active in a few minutes. However, it would not be a good idea to experiment with a sleeping bear, who might be rather grouchy if awakened from a cozy slumber.

The typical bear family consists of a papa, a mama and a baby

The story of Goldilocks is not based on the real facts of bear life.

Male and female bears make loving and devoted couples during the mating season, but afterwards the female bear separates herself from the male and goes off alone to bear her young. Thereafter, she raises her cubs without the father. If he did come around, he would be driven off by the protective mother. The typical bear family is made up of a mama and a baby (or babies), but no papa.

Are there any animal fathers who raise their young? In some species of marmosets — small monkeys — the female hands its babies over to the father immediately after birth. Except for suckling, the father does all the work of raising the young ones.

The no-longer-welcome papa bear

Bulls charge anything red

The color red is said to be irritating to a bull. The animal is thought to become especially enraged when a red object — a piece of cloth, for example — is moved about.

Actually, bulls cannot see colors. While not all animals have as yet been tested for color blindness, it seems that humans, apes and monkeys are the only mammals able to see colors.

If the bull does not become enraged at the sight of a red cloth, why is it used in bullfighting? The bullfighter, whether he is aware of it or not, is really waving a red cape around more to excite the audience than the bull. Human beings are very responsive to the color red. It is a bright color; it is the color of blood; it is a color associated with danger.

As for the bull, what excites him is not the color of the cloth, but its motion. Waving a green towel or a pair of yellow pajamas would excite him just about as much.

The buffalo roamed North America

The "American buffalo" is not a buffalo. It is a bison, which is related to the buffalo but does not quite qualify as one. The only true buffaloes are found in Africa and Asia.

Antelopes are found in the American West

"Where the deer and the antelope play" is not out West. No species of true antelope exists in North America.

The "antelope" referred to in the song "Home on the Range" is the pronghorn (or prongbuck), an animal with no close relative among the other hoofed creatures. This animal combines some of the features of the goat, sheep, giraffe, antelope and deer. When European explorers and settlers first saw these interesting animals, they took them for antelopes. Later, when zoologists examined pronghorns more closely, they found them to be different from the antelopes.

According to the theory of evolution, man developed from the apes

The theory of evolution developed by Charles Darwin (1809-1882) does not state that man developed from the apes. What the theory does say is that both man and the apes had a common ancestor. From this common ancestor, apes and man took separate evolutionary paths. One did not come from the other.

A common ancestor

Gorillas are brutal animals

The gorilla is commonly thought to be a scaled-down version of King Kong, a beast that attacks without reason or warning. Nothing could be further from the truth. Actually the gorilla is a shy, withdrawn, moody animal that prefers to avoid dangerous encounters. It will not rush at an intruder unless it feels threatened and is unable to escape the situation. If an attack is provoked, it usually consists of a swipe with its powerful arm or a single bite, and then a quick retreat.

The gorilla walks on its hind legs

Gorillas are more "four-legged" than two-legged. They move about on all fours, using the knuckles of their hands for support in front. Seldom, and then only briefly, do they stand or move in an upright position.

The kangaroo is the only animal with a pouch

A tiny baby peeking from the safety of its mother's pouch has come to be identified with the kangaroo, but at least 17 other marsupials (pouched mammals) exist, among them the koala, opossum, wombat, bandicoot, and even a species of mouse.

Pigs are dirty animals

The pig's reputation as a dirty animal is undeserved. Before domestication, the pig was a forest-roaming animal. Today, confined by man in crowded, often dirty conditions — usually the worst part of the farm — the pig does what it can to remain clean.

True, pigs wallow in mud if they have the opportunity, but for excellent reasons. They cool off this way, and wallowing in mud serves to rid a pig's skin of parasites and diminishes the pain of insect bites.

Pigs are also said to be disgusting because they eat garbage, but usually that is what they are fed. Dogs, too, eat leftover human food, but we do not call the dog's eating habits disgusting.

Finally, pigs are said to be greedy. "To eat like a pig" means to stuff one's self. Wrong again! Pigs eat only as much as they need to satisfy their hunger, while cows and horses sometimes become very sick by overeating if allowed unlimited quantities of foods they like.

Goats eat tin cans

Because of its huge appetite, the goat has been accused of eating tin cans. Goats will lick the labels off tin cans for the salt content or the glue, and they nibble at almost anything out of curiosity, but they will not nor can they eat shoes, clothing or tin cans.

Breakfast

The misunderstood wolf

The wolf is a ferocious animal

The wolf has long been thought to be an evil, ferocious killer by many people.

Recent scientific studies have shown that the wolf is not so ferocious, but a wary, often retiring animal with a complicated social organization. His strength is so limited, he cannot even overpower a deer without help, and prefers to attack only the weakest, oldest and sickest prey. Only occasionally does a wolf attack a lamb or calf, usually when no other food is available, although some individuals may make a habit of it. As for the notion that wolves are dangerous to humans, there is only one documented case of a wolf killing people, and that was in 1767!

Raccoon etiquette

Raccoons clean their food before eating it

The reason the raccoon prefers to put its food in water before eating it is not fully known. It will sometimes move a piece of food about in water until very little of it is left. Apparently cleanliness is not the animal's primary concern: it will slosh its food around in any water available, clean or muddy, and is often far from water at mealtime.

One explanation for this behavior is that the raccoon has no saliva in its mouth and thus needs to wet its food to avoid difficulty in chewing and swallowing. There is much disagreement about this, however.

The best explanation is that the raccoon washes the food it catches in streams and lakes in order to remove any sand or mud or, in the case of amphibians such as frogs and salamanders, to eliminate the unpleasant secretions on their skins. Moreover, since the raccoon is an inquisitive animal with a highly developed sense of touch, perhaps it also wants to feel and investigate the nature of its food before eating it.

The mongoose is immune to cobra poison

It is said that the mongoose fights the cobra so bravely because it is immune to the snake's venom. In fact, the mongoose is not immune to the cobra's bite, and depends only on its speed and cunning in killing the cobra.

A rabbit should be lifted by its ears

No, this is a cruel way to lift a rabbit. A rabbit's ears are particularly sensitive. They are not designed to support the weight of its body, and injury is especially likely if the animal is old and heavy.

The best way to lift a rabbit is to grasp the loose skin above the shoulders with one hand and to support its rump with the other.

Rabbits are silent animals

Rabbits seldom make a sound, true enough, but they are not voiceless. When in danger and particularly when seized by predators, they often emit loud, heart-rending screams.

While some animals do not use their voices frequently, biologists think that all higher animals can make some sort of sound.

Rabbits can be noisy

The rabbit and the hare are the same

Although the rabbit and the hare are often thought to be identical, particularly in the United States, biologists use the names to refer to two different animals. Perhaps the most obvious difference between the two is the larger size of the hare, its ears and hind legs in particular. Rabbits, unlike hares, live in communal underground burrows, called warrens. The hare builds only a crude, simple nest on the ground and the young are born fully furred and with open eyes, whereas rabbits are born blind, hairless and helpless in a more elaborate underground nest. On the basis of these traits, the jackrabbit and snowshoe rabbit of North America are true hares, while the so-called Belgian hare is really a true rabbit. The cottontail, common in the eastern United States, does not fall neatly into either group but resembles the rabbit more than the hare.

All rodents are small

Not so. The largest member of the rodent family, the capybara, is about four feet (1.2 m) in length and weighs as much as 150 pounds (68 kg). This animal lives near streams and rivers in Central and South America and swims expertly. Its jaws and teeth are extremely strong, able to cut through a metal bar.

Beavers use their tails as trowels

Children's books sometimes show beavers piling heaps of mud on their broad flat tails and then using their tails as a plasterer uses a trowel to fill holes and cracks in their dams and lodges.

Beavers use their tails in a variety of ways. They use them as rudders in swimming and as props to support them when they sit on their haunches gnawing trees. A beaver also uses its tail to warn other beavers of danger, slapping it flat against the surface of the water to produce a loud splash. As for the notion that beavers use their tails as trowels, it is pure make-believe.

Beavers are expert lumbermen

Many stories are told of how the clever beaver can chew on a tree in such a way that it falls exactly where he wants it to fall. The fact is that the beaver will gnaw a tree on the side it can get to most easily and has no sense of where the tree will fall.

Timber!

Porcupines shoot their quills at their enemies

It is not true that the porcupine, when harassed, shoots its quills at its adversary, but it's easy to see how this misconception got started. The porcupine usually defends itself with a sudden lash of its tail. Since its quills are loosely attached to its skin, if the tail misses its target some quills may fly out. Apart from this, the porcupine cannot throw or shoot its quills at its enemies.

The North American porcupine has as many as 30,000 quills, each about four inches (10.2 cm) long and tapered to a needle-sharp point. The surface of the quill is smooth except for an area just below the tip, where a band of tiny barbs is located. Each band has many barbs, which lie against the quill and point backwards along its shaft. When the quill is driven into the victim, the warmth and moisture of the flesh cause the tiny barbs to swell and become firmly anchored. Because the barbs are pointed backwards, the quill cannot be pulled out without also ripping some flesh out with it. The more the victim struggles to dislodge it, the deeper it penetrates, and if the quill pierces a vital organ the animal may die. Wolves, bears and mountain lions have been found dead with many porcupine quills embedded in their flesh.

Groundhogs can predict the weather

This superstition is thought to have begun in Europe, where it was applied to the hedgehog. When the Pilgrims came to the New World, they brought this bit of folklore with them and applied it to the groundhog.

The groundhog, or woodchuck, hibernates in its burrow during the winter months. According to the superstition, the animal comes out of its burrow on the second day of February ("Groundhog Day") and looks around. If the sky is cloudy and the groundhog cannot see its shadow, it ends its hibernation and begins foraging for food. This is supposed to mean that the weather will be mild for the remainder of the winter. However, if the weather is clear and the sun is shining, the groundhog sees its shadow and scurries back into its burrow — a sure sign, according to the myth, that six more weeks of cold weather are ahead.

There is, of course, not one bit of evidence to support this belief. Why, then, do newspapers repeat the story about the groundhog year after year? Precisely because it is such a good story. Articles about cute little animals are always popular. Reporters have even been known to poke sticks down the burrow of the woodchuck on February 2nd, to make it come out of its burrow so that its picture could be taken.

Flying squirrels fly

Flying squirrels have folds of skin between their front and hind legs. As the legs are extended sideways, each fold of skin is stretched into a flat surface, forming "wings" which enable the squirrel to take long, sailing leaps from one point in a tree to a lower one. Flying squirrels are really gliding, not flying, as their "wings" do not flap. Bats are the only mammals that actually fly.

The common house mouse is native to the United States

The common mouse found in American homes originally inhabited Europe and central Asia. The field mouse or meadow vole, on the other hand, is a true native of the United States. It can be readily distinguished from the house mouse by its heavier body, beady eyes, shorter tail and lighter belly. Field mice are so named because they prefer to live outdoors and are seldom found in houses.

Mice are quiet

The phrase "quiet as a mouse" is inaccurate. Mice are far from silent. Investigators have found that in addition to squeaking, some mice make musical sounds similar to the twittering, chirping and warbling of small birds. Such noises are made by a variety of mice, including the common house mouse.

Mice are particularly fond of cheese

Sorry, but all those cartoons that show mice gobbling up cheese as if it were their favorite food, are wrong. Mice do not prefer cheese and often will not touch it if any other food is available.

Moles eat vegetable matter

The average gardener considers the mole to be a nasty pest that eats roots, bulbs and plants. However, the mole is innocent of such things; it is strictly carnivorous, devouring earthworms, grubs and various insects. Most of the damage to bulbs, tubers, roots and seeds is done by field mice which invade the tunnels made by the mole.

In order to maintain its high metabolic rate, the mole must eat an enormous amount of food to keep it going. It burrows through the earth almost continuously in search of food, and some tunnels extend for hundreds of feet. As unhappy as the gardener may be about mole tunnels, the tunnels do aerate and thus improve the soil, and moles rid a garden of many destructive insects and grubs. On the other hand, when a mole, burrowing just below the surface of the ground, enters a lawn, the earth and grass above the tunnel are pushed up, and the lawn may soon become crisscrossed by long, winding, unsightly ridges.

The mole is blind

The mole is commonly believed to be blind. Actually, it can see, if only poorly. Many species are only able to distinguish light from darkness. In most species, the younger the animal, the better the vision. As the animal ages, its fur and skin begin to cover the eyes, and thus the eyes of most adult moles are completely hidden or nearly so.

Bats are blind

The common expression "as blind as a bat" is simply not factual.

Bats are nocturnal; that is, they usually sleep during the day and are active at night. If disturbed and forced to leave their dark caves, they are only briefly inconvenienced. It takes the bat a while to adjust to the glare of daylight, but after that the eyes of bats are as good as those of many other animals.

Bats have a built-in radar system

How do bats find their way in the dark? Bats emit supersonic sounds — cries so high-pitched that the human ear cannot hear them. However, the bats can. The sounds are bounced off objects and are reflected back to the ears of the bat, telling the animal what objects are around it from moment to moment. This enables the bat to fly around without bumping into anything even in total darkness. A blindfolded bat, set loose in a dark room cross-strung with piano wires, can fly around at top speed and never touch a wire, but if its ears are plugged up, it blunders hopelessly because it cannot hear the guiding echo of its supersonic voice.

However, is this really a radar system? Radar bounces electromagnetic waves off objects to determine their location. The system used by the bat is based on sound; that is, it is a sonar system. The bat, then, uses a sonar rather than a radar system. Many people confuse the two.

Birds

Birds sing to express their happiness

Human beings may sing out of happiness, but birds do not. Bird songs are actually part of a complex communication system that is used most during the breeding season.

A male bird sings primarily for two reasons: to announce that he has established for himself a territory that other males of his species should stay away from, and to attract a mate.

The females of most song bird species do not sing; a few do, but these do not sing as much as or as well as the males. The female canary, for example, has a weaker, shorter and less appealing song than the male.

Thus, bird song is an important part of courtship and related activity, not a method by which the bird announces its happiness to the world.

Birds have small brains

A person with low intelligence is often said to be "bird-brained" because it is believed that birds have tiny brains. Actually, the brain of the bird is large and heavy in proportion to its body weight. Moreover, some birds — crows, for example — are quite intelligent.

Birds must flap their wings to stay in the air

Condors, buzzards and hawks often fly at great heights and can remain aloft for hours on end without any movement of their wings. These birds are able to ride on rising air currents and take advantage of changes in air currents by slight motions of the body, head and tail. This kind of flight is similar to the flight of a kite, and is called soaring.

Certain birds of the vulture type depend so much on air currents in flying that they prefer to perch in trees on still, windless days when soaring would be too difficult.

Rest now, soar later

Leader of the flock

One bird always leads the flock

It is commonly assumed that one bird leads a flock of birds in flight. The leader is thought to be the oldest or the most experienced or the strongest of the birds. This is not the case.

Observe any flock of birds, and you will note that the flock periodically breaks formation and reassembles a short distance beyond. Each time the flock does so, a different individual assumes the position at the head of the flock and becomes the new leader.

Birds can only fly forwards

Anyone who thinks that birds can only fly forwards has not seen the hummingbird in action. No other bird in the world can match the flying ability of this tiny bird. Hummingbirds can hover in one spot, move up, down, forwards, backwards and even sideways. How does the hummingbird do this? In addition to having an extremely rapid wing beat — as many as 75 beats a second — the hummingbird is able to rotate its wings at the socket during each beat. The wings of the hummingbird are like the blades of a helicopter, which change pitch as needed, making the helicopter extremely maneuverable.

Adult birds never lose the ability to fly

After raising their young, most birds go through a period of moulting, shedding their feathers and growing new ones. They lose only a few feathers at a time from each wing, and new feathers quickly grow in to replace those lost. The bird is able to fly at all times.

It is not well known, however, that most waterfowl lose their ability to fly during moulting. Swans, geese, ducks and rails, among others, shed all their flight feathers at once. These birds may be totally incapable of flight for several weeks.

Sleeping birds sometimes fall from their perches

Impossible!

There are tendons in a bird's foot that extend from the toes past the ankle joint and up the leg to the muscles above. When a bird alights on a twig, its weight bends this joint and the tendons are stretched and pulled taut, which in turn makes the toes curl and grasp the perch firmly. Thus a bird is in no danger of losing its grip on its perch during sleep.

All birds build nests

No. Quite a few birds do not. Those birds which lay eggs on the ground often do not build nests. Many shore birds and terns merely scrape a slight hollow in the sand or grass into which they lay their eggs. Most parrots and many owls nest in tree holes that are lined with little or no nest material.

Some birds build no nests because they live as parasites on other birds. The cowbird, for example, lays its eggs in the nests of other birds, tricking other birds into rearing its young.

Only female birds incubate eggs

Don't you believe it. Many kinds of brooding behavior may be observed among birds. In some, the female alone sits on the eggs. In others, the male does all the brooding; three examples of this are the rhea, kiwi and phalarope. In still others, both sexes take turns incubating the eggs. It has been estimated that in well over half of bird families both sexes share the task of incubation.

A duckling is dunked

Birds do not carry their babies around

A mother cat carrying her kittens from place to place is a common sight. If you said birds never do this sort of thing, you would be wrong.

An alarmed mother woodcock often tucks her chick between her thighs, clamps her legs together, and flies off to a safer place. A duck called the hooded merganser nests in tree holes that are sometimes high above the ground and some distance from water. When its ducklings are ready to leave the nest, it often carries them in its bill, one by one, to the nearest lake or marsh. Wood ducks have been observed doing this, too.

Ostriches bury their heads in the sand

When an ostrich 8 feet (2.4 m) tall senses danger, it often drops down and stretches its long neck along the ground to make itself less visible, but it never buries its head in the sand. If the danger becomes threatening, the ostrich rises and runs away. It can attain speeds of up to 50 miles (80.5 km) per hour. It can also put up a pretty good fight. The ostrich is capable of inflicting serious wounds with its sharp toes and powerful kick. Men and even horses are reported to have been killed by the blows.

Bald eagles are bald

No, the bald eagle is not bald. This species of eagle, the symbol of the United States, has a dark head when young. As the eagle matures, the dark head feathers are replaced by white head feathers that extend over its neck.

All bald eagles are protected by law. However, many are shot every year simply because they make big targets for hunters. Pollution and insecticides are also killing this majestic bird. The number of bald eagles is decreasing and the species is in danger of extinction.

"As straight as the crow flies"

This is one of those common expressions which, when investigated, turn out to be misleading. Crows often do not fly in a straight line, preferring to meander widely or to follow a zigzag course.

The un-loony loon

The loon is a crazy bird

The expression "crazy as a loon" gives that bird a reputation that is undeserved. Although its call sounds crazy, the loon is actually one of the most intelligent birds.

Penguins are found at the North Pole

When people think of penguins, they think of funny little black-and-white creatures who live in cold, icy regions. Since the North Pole is cold, they assume the penguin lives there. They are wrong. The penguin lives in the Antarctic region, which includes the South Pole, as well as other parts of the Southern Hemisphere.

59

Similarly, many people think the polar bear lives at the South Pole. Actually, polar bears are found in the Arctic region, which includes the North Pole.

The owl is wise

The owl is a symbol of wisdom, but this is not accurate. Compared to many other birds, the owl is slow-witted and rather stupid.

The unwise owl

A peacock at ease

The peacock displays his tail

The beautiful fan of feathers you see is not the peacock's tail at all. These long, lovely display feathers (called a "train") grow on the lower part of the back, just above the true tail, which consists of 20 short, stiff, plain-colored feathers. When the peacock wishes to put on his display (to show off), the true tail lifts, fans out, and raises and supports the display feathers.

Reptiles and Amphibians

Prehistoric man and dinosaurs once lived together

Despite cartoon strips and television shows which sometimes depict man and dinosaurs co-existing, humans and dinosaurs could not have lived together.

Most estimates place the origin of man at 2-4 million years ago. The last of the dinosaurs disappeared more than 60 million years ago, at the end of the Mesozoic era. Hence, by the time man arrived on earth, the dinosaurs had been extinct for millions of years.

The dinosaur was the largest creature that has ever lived

This may come as a surprise, but some dinosaurs were no larger than a chicken. Other dinosaurs, of course, were large indeed. *Brontosaurus* was over 60 feet (18 m) long and weighed between 30 and 40 tons (27 to 36 metric tons). *Diplodocus*, another dinosaur, had a length of up to 87 feet (26.5 m), but a weight of only 12 tons (10.8 metric tons). Most massive of the large dinosaurs was *Brachiosaurus*, which stood 40 feet (12 m) tall when it held its neck erect, was 80 feet (24 m) long and weighed 60 tons (54 metric tons).

However, none of these prehistoric creatures were anywhere near the size and weight of today's largest animal, the blue or sulphur-bottom whale. The blue whale may reach 110 feet (33.5 m) in length, and can weigh up to 175 tons (158 metric tons), the equivalent of 30 elephants and about three times the mass of the largest dinosaur.

Dinosaurs came in all sizes

Snakes are slippery and slimy

People who say that snakes are slippery and slimy have never touched one. The skin of a snake is cool, dry and remarkably clean. You will not see a dirty snake, either in the wild or in captivity. The reason is that the skin sheds water and mud and, being dry and smooth, does not readily pick up dirt.

Snake charmers make the cobra dance

Snake charmers claim they are able to put a snake, usually a cobra, into a trance. As the snake charmer plays his music, the cobra supposedly sways ("dances") to its rhythm and comes under the hypnotic power of the charmer.

Scientists doubt this is what really happens. The cobra is not hypnotized by the sound of the music because, like all snakes, it is deaf.

How, then, does the snake charmer make the cobra move as it does? Since snakes are very sensitive to vibrations, he may arouse the cobra and get it to rear its head by tapping his foot as he plays the music. Also, as the snake charmer and his flute move from side to side, the cobra is attracted by this and follows each movement intently. If the snake charmer did not move, the snake would not sway either.

The music, spoken commands and other antics of the snake charmer are really intended to charm the human spectators, not the snake.

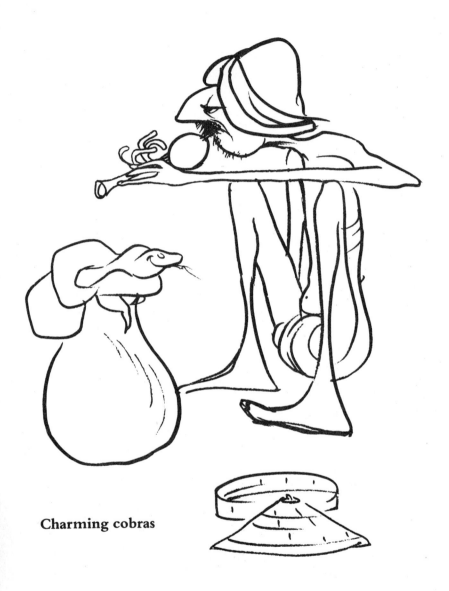

Charming cobras

The boa constrictor kills by crushing its victims

The boa constrictor (and other constricting snakes) does not crush its victims to death. Instead, it quickly throws three or four coils around the animal it has caught and tightens its grip each time its prey exhales. Soon the victim cannot breathe and death follows. Rather than being crushed to death, the victim dies of suffocation.

Crocodile tears are false tears

Crocodiles often do "shed crocodile tears" when feeding, but not out of mock pity for the victims they are devouring. The tears are simply an automatic reflex which occurs when they open their jaws wide, just as our eyes sometimes become watery when we yawn.

Crocodile tears

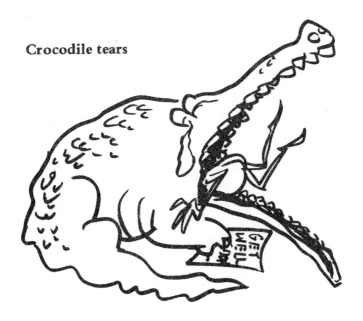

The rattlesnake always warns before it strikes

Many snakes vibrate their tails when excited or threatened, but only the rattlesnake is equipped with a rattle. The tail of the rattlesnake usually vibrates about 48 cycles per second and may be heard up to a distance of 100 feet (30.5 m).

Can the rattlesnake always be counted on to rattle before it strikes, as many people suppose? No. Many victims have discovered, to their misfortune, that the rattlesnake may strike without the slightest warning. Furthermore, when a rattler does rattle, it is not a conscious attempt by the snake to warn an intruder, but simply the reaction of a nervous, angry rattlesnake.

Does the rattlesnake always take the time to coil

before it strikes? Usually, but not always. The rattlesnake can strike without first coiling and often does when suddenly stepped on or otherwise surprised by a human or other animal.

The chameleon changes color to match its background

Chameleons do undergo rapid changes of color, but this has nothing to do with the color of their surroundings.

Cells in the chameleon's skin contain pigments that are involved in these color changes. When the chameleon becomes angry or frightened, nerve impulses sent to the color cells cause the colors to darken. Heat and cold, sunlight and darkness also affect the color of the chameleon.

Thus, temperature, light changes and the chameleon's state of mind are responsible for its color changes.

Toads cause warts

There is not the slightest evidence that toads cause or have anything at all to do with warts. Wart-like bumps on the body of the toad may resemble those on the human body, but medical scientists say that human warts are caused by a virus and are often associated with poor hygiene.

However, the skins of many toads are covered with a secretion that can cause irritation if it comes into contact with the eyes, mouth or a cut on the skin. These animals should therefore be handled cautiously.

The horned toad is a toad

The horned toad is misnamed; it is a lizard. The remarkable feature of this small desert reptile is that it often squirts a thin stream of blood from the corner of each eye when it feels threatened or otherwise becomes excited. How this happens is not entirely clear, but one theory is that the lizard's excitement brings on high blood pressure which causes the delicate capillaries (tiny blood vessels) in its eyes to rupture.

A squirt of a lizard

Fish and Other Water Animals

All fish have scales

Most, but not all, fish have scales. The catfish, for example, has no scales. Nor are fish born with scales. The scales sprout later, from under the skin. Does a fish grow more scales as it increases in size? No, the scales remain the same in number; each separate scale just grows larger.

Fish swim with their fins

The impression that fish swim with their fins is a common one, the result, perhaps, of observing how humans and other animals swim and assuming that fish swim in a similar way. Actually, fish propel themselves forward by moving their tails from side to side. The fins are used for steering and stabilizing.

Fish can't drown

If "drowning" is taken to mean suffocation due to a lack of oxygen, then fish do drown.

Fish breathe by taking oxygen from the water. If the oxygen in the water is used up, the fish must either move to other waters where the oxygen supply is adequate, or die of suffocation. Millions of fish, in fact, die from suffocation each year. The problem is growing more serious as water pollution destroys oxygen supplies in a large part of the earth's waters.

Fish die out of water

There are fish with the ability to remain out of water for long periods of time, and which can clumsily "walk" considerable distances. The walking catfish of Florida (originally from Thailand) are multiplying so rapidly that they are becoming a nuisance, and the climbing perch of India is well known. In other parts of the world, fish such as gobies, blennies and serpent-heads move through grass or mud from one body of water to another when necessary.

In addition to gills, all walking fish are equipped with breathing systems that enable them to take oxygen from the air. These fish "walk" awkwardly at best. The fins are used as legs, although they wriggle forward primarily by vigorous movements of their tails.

Some biologists believe that these fish are in the process of becoming land animals; that eventually, after slowly changing over a very long period of time, they will become adapted to living on land only and will not be able to swim like fish again.

The whale is the largest fish

Ask people to name the largest fish, and many will say the whale. The whale is the biggest creature in the sea, of course, but it is not a fish. It is a mammal.

The largest fish is the whale shark. A specimen between 55 and 65 feet (17 and 20 m) in length and weighing at least 40 tons (36,240 kg) was caught in 1919. Like many whales, the whale shark feeds on plankton, tiny animal and plant organisms abundant in the sea.

Porpoises perform brilliantly in water shows

Almost all the trained "porpoises" that entertain audiences at water shows are not porpoises at all, but dolphins. Usually, bottle-nosed dolphins are used for this purpose.

The dolphin is one of nature's most intelligent animals. These friendly, playful mammals are genuinely fond of human beings, and can be trained to imitate human speech to some extent. They are known to rescue one of their group that is injured or sick, supporting it at the surface so that it can breathe. There have also been reports of dolphins saving the lives of drowning persons by pushing them to shore. It is not known whether the animal is being consciously helpful or only playful in doing so.

The shark is the dolphin's main enemy. A shark is either evaded with great speed and tricky maneuvering or, if encountered by a school of dolphins, battered to death with the dolphins' hard noses.

The talented dolphin

The shark causes more injuries to man than any other fish

Not true. The stingrays, in fact, cause more injuries to man each year than all other species of fish combined. It is estimated that in the United States there are 1,000 cases of injury by stingrays each year. While the sting of the ray is usually not fatal, it can be extremely painful.

None of the various species of stingrays, which are related to the shark, are known to attack man. Almost every reported case of injury involved a victim who stepped on a stingray by mistake. Injuries have also resulted from attempts to handle these creatures.

Stingrays are mostly shallow-water creatures that often lie partially submerged under sand and mud. Because their flattened bodies are the same color as the bottom, they are difficult to see. The unsuspecting wader who steps on the ray is lashed by its tail, which is swiftly brought up and forward with great power. The tail not only cuts the victim, but injects poison into the wound.

Stingrays, when seen, should be left alone. One found in a swimming area can be made to move on by prodding it with a long pole (but never with hands or feet).

The electric eel is a true eel

The electric eel is not really an eel; it is more closely related to the carp and catfish than to the eels. One difference between the two is that a true eel breathes in water, while an electric eel cannot. The gills of the electric eel are simply too primitive to obtain oxygen from water, and it must rise to the surface periodically to gulp air. The walls of its mouth are lined with a rich network of blood vessels which enable the electric eel to take oxygen directly from the air.

Contrary to what many people suppose, the electric eel is not unique in its ability to generate electricity. There are many species of fish that can do this. However, the electric eel can generate a greater electric current than any other electric fish. The average electrical discharge is 350 volts, but it can release a charge as high as 600 volts. Fortunately the amperage is low, about 1 ampere, and as a result the charge is powerful enough to stun a man but not to kill him.

It is not generally realized that the electric discharge of the eel is used not only to stun its prey and ward off its enemies, but also as a navigational device. It allows the electric eel to make its way safely through the muddy waters in which it often lives. Small electric currents are constantly sent out and reflected by objects in the eel's path, and the animal is thus able to sense the nature of its surroundings. This, of course, is exactly what a sophisticated radar system does. The electric eel not only generates electricity, but also operates a true radar system.

The octopus squeezes its victim to death

Under no circumstances does the octopus strangle or crush its victims with its arms. The arms (tentacles) are used solely for holding the victim so that it can be bitten by the parrot-like beak of the octopus. Many octopus species are venomous, injecting poisonous saliva into the wound made by the beak. So far as is known, however, only one octopus, the small blue-ringed octopus found off Australia, is capable of killing humans.

A large octopus may look threatening but is seldom a real danger. Octopuses (octopi) are shy and prefer to hide in the safety of rocks and crevices, escaping the notice of their enemies by an amazing ability to change color and blend in with their surroundings.

The many tales of giant octopuses attacking men and boats are just fantasy. If there is any foundation to such stories, it is the giant squid and not the octopus that is probably involved. The giant squid is not only larger than the octopus, it is also a more aggressive creature. Specimens of giant squid have reached 55 feet (17 m) and weighed over 4,000 pounds (1,812 kg).

Horseshoe crabs are crabs

Horseshoe crabs are not crabs; they are not even crustaceans. That is, horseshoe crabs, despite their appearance, are not closely related to such water creatures as the shrimp, crab, lobster and crayfish. Horseshoe crabs, instead, are related to the arachnids. The nearest relatives of the horseshoe crab are such creatures as the mite, tick, scorpion and spider.

Horseshoe crabs are called "living fossils," and with good reason. They evolved 150 million years ago, and have not changed since then.

Flying fish really fly

Glide, yes; fly, no. The idea that these fish "flap their wings" in true flight is wrong. The enlarged pectoral fins of an airborne flying fish remain rigid, and thus the flying fish cannot be said to fly like birds.

This is not to deny the remarkable ability of the flying fish to take to the air. When pursued by larger fish, it uses its powerful tail to build up enough speed in the water and then takes off, gliding as far as 200 yards (183 m) in the air before dropping back into the sea.

A dramatic escape

Insects, Spiders and Related Creatures

Insects have red blood

No, the red blood you may see on a squashed insect, such as a mosquito, is actually blood the insect has sucked from a red-blooded animal. The greenish color of the squashed bodies of other insects is from the undigested vegetable matter in the digestive tract. Insect blood is colorless, or faintly yellow.

Dragonflies are dangerous

For some unknown reason, the dragonfly with its huge transparent wings is thought to sting. It has no stingers and is in all ways completely harmless. These interesting insects fly with great speed and have the unusual ability to dart backwards and forwards without turning. On the whole they are beneficial to man, feeding on mosquitoes, gnats and other small insects which they capture and devour while in flight.

The wings of butterflies are colored

Not exactly. The wings of butterflies have no color. All those beautiful colors and designs are produced by thousands of tiny colored scales on the surfaces of the wings. If the wings of butterflies (and moths) are touched when the insects are handled, these scales fall off very easily, revealing a transparent wing underneath.

The praying mantis is protected by United States law

Because the praying mantis is so beneficial to man, it is commonly believed that this insect is protected by law. It is not. Currently, no insect species is protected by U.S. law.

The mantis eats insect pests

The clothes moth eats wool

A moth known as the "clothes moth" is commonly believed to eat holes in clothing, furs and even carpets. However, the moth itself is not responsible for such damage.

The moth eats nothing at all. It exists solely for the purpose of forming and depositing eggs. The eggs then hatch into larvae — a stage in the insect's development in which it resembles a small worm or caterpillar — and it is these larvae that eat holes in the clothing. The larvae later develop into moths and the cycle is repeated.

Do moth balls help? Yes, they keep adult moths away. However, they do not kill eggs or larvae already present. Storage of clothes in cedar chests also helps to protect them against damage by moth larvae.

Bees gather honey from flowers

The bee crawling into a blossom does not find honey, but a thin, sweet liquid called nectar. The bee sucks up this nectar, swallows it, and flies back to the hive where it "throws up" (regurgitates) the nectar. Younger bees in the hive then swallow the nectar and it is regurgitated once more. The nectar is converted into a thin honey by chemical processes in the bodies of the bees. After the thin honey is deposited in the hive it gradually thickens by evaporation until it becomes the honey we know and use.

The common housefly bites

The housefly cannot bite or chew anything. Its mouth parts are soft and fleshy, designed for sucking liquids only. However, the stable fly, which is similar in appearance and also visits human dwellings, has mouth parts formed especially for piercing flesh. Other biting flies include horseflies, deerflies and black flies.

To eat, the common housefly first deposits some liquid from a previous meal to dissolve the food it wishes to dine on, a lump of sugar let us say, then sucks up the resulting sweet liquid.

All mosquitoes live on blood

The males don't! They lack the proper mouth parts for piercing animal skin and sucking blood. Only the female mosquito eats blood. When it is unable to obtain animal blood, the female, like the male, feeds on plant juices, nectar and fruit.

Shellac comes from pine trees

Shellac comes from the lac insect, which inhabits the tropical forests of southern Asia. The female lac insect secretes a thick coat of wax or lac which covers its body and is also deposited on nearby twigs and branches. Both the insect and the twigs are collected by natives and the lac is processed to produce shellac.

Most shellac comes from India and Burma.

A millipede has its problems

A centipede has a hundred legs

Sorry, but the common house centipede (*centi*- meaning one hundred) has 30 legs. Garden centipedes have 21 pairs of legs. Furthermore, there are others with well over 100 legs.

Does the millipede (*milli*- meaning one thousand) have a thousand legs? No. The maximum number of legs is slightly more than 200, and most common millipedes have only 30 to 60 pairs of legs.

The spider is an insect

The spider may look like an insect, but it is not one. The spider belongs to a group of creatures called arachnids.

How do spiders differ from insects? An insect has three pairs of legs; the spider has four pairs. An insect body is divided into three parts — the head, the thorax or middle part, and the abdomen at the rear — while the body of the spider is divided into two parts, the head and thorax being joined. Growing out of the head of an insect are two sense organs called antennae; spiders have no antennae. Spiders have simple eyes, often eight in number, whereas insects have several simple eyes and two compound eyes made up of many little facets for more effective sight. An insect breathes by means of small holes along its body called spiracles and air tubes called tracheae; a spider's breathing apparatus consists of many leaf-like plates called book lungs. Finally, spiders have no wings, while insects usually have two pairs.

The closest relatives of the spiders are the scorpions, ticks and mites, not the insects.

The tarantula is dangerous to man

Death from the bite of a giant tarantula is extremely rare.

The tarantula may look dangerous, but it is basically sluggish, easily tamed and seldom bites humans. There are many species of tarantula, some with bodies 3 inches (7.6 cm) long and 10 inches (25 cm) across with legs extended. Their bite is painful but has little other effect on man; a bee sting may hurt more and is frequently more dangerous.

A pet tarantula?!

Spider webs are delicate

The thread spun by the spider may look weak, but actually spider's silk is stronger for its size than any other fiber found in nature. It is very elastic, stretching one-fifth of its length without breaking. The tensile strength of spider silk is greater than that of steel.

The mighty spider web

science

Listening to a seashell

As you listen to a shell, you can hear the roar of the sea

When you hold a seashell close to your ear, the noise you hear is a combination of ordinary sounds coming from outside the shell in your immediate surroundings. Because of the peculiar shape of the shell and the smoothness of its interior, the sound from outside the shell is echoed and re-echoed as the air inside the hollow shell vibrates. These echoes blend together to produce the roaring sound you hear. Among the sounds picked up and amplified is the sound of blood rushing through your ear.

The sky is blue

The sky is not blue; it has no color of its own. The blue color of the sky is the result of what happens to sunlight as it travels through the atmosphere.

Sunlight is a combination of all the colors in the rainbow. As it passes through the atmosphere, millions of small particles suspended in the air scatter the sunlight. Blue light, since it has a short wavelength, is more readily scattered than reds and yellows, which have longer wavelengths. The sky is lit up, so to speak, by the blue light contained in sunlight.

The ocean is blue for the same reason. The blue of the sea is caused by the scattering of sunlight by tiny suspended particles in the water. The emptier the water, the bluer it appears. The presence of microscopic plant life makes the water green, brown or even reddish.

The rocket is a modern invention

The rocket was invented by the Chinese as far back as 1200 A.D., a century before the cannon. The early rocket consisted of a simple tube into which black gunpowder was poured as a propellant. The first recorded military use of rockets was in the siege of Kaifeng, China in 1232.

The rocket spread to Europe, where its use was recorded in 1258 in Cologne, Germany. Soon, however, the more accurate cannon largely replaced the rocket, which thereafter was used mainly on ships.

In the late 18th century, military interest in rockets was revived and improvements were made in their design, especially by the British.

Most lightning victims are instantly killed

On the contrary, most people struck by lightning recover completely, and many more would survive if bystanders came to their assistance instead of assuming them to be dead.

People hit by lightning often stop breathing, and artificial respiration should be given as soon as possible. Once the victim's breathing resumes, he may be examined and treated for burns. Sometimes the heart stops, but the victim can often be revived by external massage.

Another reason many lightning victims do not receive immediate assistance by bystanders is the completely mistaken notion that a person struck by lightning retains electricity and can give a shock. The victim's body is perfectly safe to touch.

Lightning <u>can</u> strike twice

Lightning never strikes twice in the same place

This is not true. Lightning can and does repeatedly strike the same object — be it a lone tree in a field or a lightning rod on the roof of a building. The spire atop the Empire State Building is struck as often as 50 times a year. Are the people in the building at the time hurt in any way by the lightning? No, they are not even aware that the building is being struck.

The greatest explosion of all time was produced by the hydrogen bomb

In 1470 B.C. the volcanic island of Thera in the Aegean Sea exploded in what was probably the biggest, most devastating upheaval in history. However, because it occurred so long ago, little about it is known for certain.

The most powerful explosion in modern history — with 26 times the power of the hydrogen bomb — occurred on August 27, 1883, on the volcanic island of Krakatoa, located in the Sunda Strait between Java and Sumatra. After two days of violent eruption, only a small piece of the island remained. A great volume of rock and other material was thrown as high as 34 miles (55 km) into the air, and a huge tidal wave perhaps a hundred feet high killed tens of thousands of people in villages in the area. The thunderous explosion was heard in Australia, 2,250 miles (3,621 km) away. For the next year, many parts of the world experienced very brilliant sunrises and sunsets as clouds of volcanic dust and ash from the Krakatoa eruption continued to circle the globe.

What is left of the Krakatoa volcano still erupts occasionally — with much less force than the 1883 blast.

Steam is visible

Everyone can see mist rising from boiling water, but strictly speaking, that is not steam. Steam is not only invisible, it is not even wet. It ceases to be steam and becomes a visible mist when water droplets are formed by a drop in temperature.

Look carefully at the spout of a boiling tea kettle, and you will observe that the steam is invisible as it comes from the spout. It becomes visible only when the steam is exposed to the cooler air an inch or so away from the spout. This mist is the result of condensation of steam into tiny water droplets when it meets the cooler air in the room.

The humming sound of telephone wires is due to the flow of electric current through them

Telephone wires strung on poles sometimes give off a humming sound. This noise is produced not by electric current as it flows through the wires, but by the wind. The wires, set in motion by the wind, vibrate very much like the strings of a guitar or a harp when plucked. The pitch and volume of the sound depend on the direction and velocity of the wind, the tightness of the wires, and the distance between the telephone poles.

An electric fan cools the air

No fan makes the temperature in the air drop. In fact, strictly speaking, the electric fan tends to increase the temperature of a room because of the heat produced by the motor. The fan's cooling effect is due to the fact that body perspiration evaporates more rapidly in circulating air than in stagnant air. It is this increased rate of evaporation that cools you, because evaporation is a cooling process.

The steam engine is a modern invention

The steam engine is assumed to be a modern invention. The names of James Watt (1736-1819) and Thomas Newcomen (1663-1729) come to mind, and a few people may be aware that the first steam engine was patented by Thomas Savery (1650?-1715) in 1698. It is not generally realized, however, that the steam engine has been around much longer than this.

A man named Hero of Alexandria, who probably lived in that Egyptian city about the first century A.D., invented a primitive steam engine called the aeolipile. This basically two-part device consisted of a boiler in which water was heated to produce steam, and a suspended hollow ball. The steam, guided into the ball, escaped from two nozzles on opposite sides of the ball, making it revolve. Hero's aeolipile was not only the first steam engine, it was also a machine illustrating the principle of jet propulsion.

Oxygen burns

When some substances combine chemically with oxygen, heat and light are given off. That is what is called burning. The oxygen itself does not burn; it only supports the burning of other substances. Pure oxygen is non-flammable.

Astronomy

Copernicus was the first to assert that the sun is the center of the solar system

Nicolaus Copernicus (1473-1543), the great Polish scientist who founded modern astronomy, is commonly thought to have been the first to argue that the sun is the center of out planetary system and that the planets, including the earth, revolve around the sun. Actually, it was Aristarchus of Samos who, in the 3rd century B.C., first developed a theory in which the sun, not the earth, held the central position in the solar system.

However, Aristarchus's analysis of the universe was not accepted by his fellow Greeks. After all, didn't their eyes show them what happened in the heavens? The sun rose in the east and set in the west, and the moon and stars turned in the sky. Everything seemed to move but the earth. Therefore, mankind continued to consider the earth to be the center of the universe, the planet around which everything in the heavens revolved. Not until Copernicus was this notion, despite initial resistance, finally abandoned.

Until Columbus proved otherwise, people thought the world was flat

Not true. As early as the sixth century B.C., Pythagoras of Greece was convinced that the earth was round. The astronomer Claudius Ptolemy in the second century A.D. noted that during an eclipse, the shadow the earth cast on the moon was round. He concluded that it was round because the earth itself was round. Ptolemy also observed that the mast of a ship approaching land is visible before the hull is, and maintained that this could happen only because the earth was spherical.

The sun is farthest from the earth in winter

It is a common but mistaken belief that it is cold in winter because then the sun is farthest from the earth. As a matter of fact, during winter the sun is closer to the earth than during any other season; it is about 3,000,000 miles (4,830,000 km) nearer the earth in the middle of winter than it is in the middle of summer.

The tilt of the earth's axis, not the varying distance of the sun from the earth, determines the change of seasons. When this tilt (slightly more than 23°) is towards the sun, as occurs in summer, the rays of the sun strike the earth more directly (and thus bring more warmth) than when the earth is inclined away from the sun, as happens in winter. (This is so only in the Northern Hemisphere; in the Southern Hemisphere the reverse is true.)

There would be no seasons as we know them if the earth's axis were vertical and not tilted. Constant summer would exist in regions near the equator, and it would always be winter in areas near the poles.

The sun remains stationary as the earth revolves around it

Every child in elementary school knows that the earth travels around the sun. The earth circles the sun at a rate of 66,500 miles (107,000 km) per hour, and makes a complete orbit every year. What many people do not know is that the sun does not stand still but is also speeding through space.

The entire solar system is revolving around the hub of our local galaxy, the Milky Way, at a tremendous rate of speed. The Milky Way, in turn, is moving even faster around the core of a cluster of galaxies. Finally, the cluster of galaxies is also moving at great speed away from other galaxy clusters.

Does anything in our universe stand still? Scientists say no, nothing.

The sun is a solid mass

It is commonly supposed that the sun consists of solid material similar to that of the earth, the basic difference between the two being that the matter of the sun is at such a high temperature that it burns and gives off light.

Actually, the sun is about 81 per cent hydrogen and 18 per cent helium, containing only about 1 per cent of heavier elements. Since both hydrogen and helium are gases, the sun is really a ball of gas rather than a solid sphere. Nevertheless, the sun is so vast that it constitutes 99.9 per cent of the mass of the entire solar system!

The moon shines

When people say the moon shines, they are not speaking correctly. The moon, having no light of its own, does not shine; it reflects the light of the sun.

Looking for Venus

The planets are visible only at night

If you know where to look in the sky, you will be able to see Venus with the naked eye in the daytime for several weeks each year. Incidentally, once in about eight years Venus at night is about twelve times as bright as Sirius, the brightest star in the skies of the Northern Hemisphere.

Shooting stars are stars

Shooting or falling stars are not stars but meteors. These masses of matter are material left behind by other bodies in the solar system, and if they enter the earth's gravitational field they fall towards the earth at tremendous speeds of 600 to 2,400 miles (966 km to 3,864 km) per hour. The enormous amount of friction that develops as a meteor plummets through the earth's atmosphere causes it to glow white with heat. When this happens it can be seen from the earth as a shooting or falling star.

A meteor fragment that reaches the ground is called a meteorite. Since all but the largest meteors burn up before they reach the earth, the vast majority of meteorites are no larger than a particle of dust. A few are quite big, however. The largest known meteorite, found in South-West Africa in 1920, weighed 132,000 pounds (59,800 kg).

Scientists estimate that hundreds of millions of meteors (both those that are visible and those that are invisible to the human eye) enter the earth's atmosphere every 24 hours. Although all but a very small number of these are mere specks by the time they reach the earth and no one has yet been killed by a falling meteorite, there is some danger to human life. In September, 1954, a woman reported being injured by a meteorite in Sylacauga, Alabama. There is also a report of a Japanese girl being hit a glancing blow by a meteorite. The Field Museum of Natural History in Chicago has an unusual exhibit: a garage roof and an automobile which in 1938 were struck and penetrated by a 3.5-pound (1.6-kg) meteorite in Illinois.

Comets and meteors are the same

Although the two are often thought to be the same, comets and meteors are quite different. A meteor, as we have seen, is a solid piece of material floating in space which, if caught in the earth's gravitational pull, enters the atmosphere at tremendous speed and heats up to white-hot temperatures. Those we see appear to us as fast-moving streaks of light across the sky.

Comets, on the other hand, are frozen chunks of matter — primarily dust, small pieces of rock and solidified gases — that develop "tails" when they approach the sun. Unlike meteors, comets do not become extremely hot; they glow because their tiny particles of matter reflect the light of the sun. Another difference is that, when a comet passes near the sun, it expands to enormous size, becoming many times the size of the earth as the sun's radiation vaporizes its frozen gases and the small solid particles of its head become widely separated. Although both comets and meteors orbit the sun, comets have huge, oval-shaped, stable orbits while those of meteors are smaller and tend to change.

Moreover, although their speed is great, comets, unlike meteors, appear to be motionless spots of light in the sky because they are so far away. Finally, comets may come relatively close to earth but have never entered the planet's atmosphere and struck its surface, while meteors sometimes do. The closest approach was that of Lexell's Comet, which in 1770 came to within 1,500,000 miles (2,413,500 km) of the earth.

The Earth

The earth is a sphere

If you ask most people, they will say the earth is perfectly round, a sphere. It is almost a sphere, but not quite. As a result of its rapid rotation, the earth bulges slightly at the equator and is somewhat flattened at the poles.

During earthquakes, people are swallowed up by the earth

During an earthquake it is very unlikely that the ground will open up, cause people to fall in and then close on its unlucky victims. Throughout recorded history, only in one instance has this happened. In 1948, during an earthquake in Fukui, Japan, a woman fell into a newly opened crack in the earth, which quickly closed in on her up to the height of her chin. She died instantly. A cow was also killed in this way during the San Francisco earthquake of 1906.

Most casualties during and immediately after earthquakes are caused by the collapse of buildings. In the great Shensi earthquake of 1556, some 830,000 Chinese died when the homes in which they lived caved in.

Keeping cool at the equator

It is hot everywhere on the equator

Not on tall mountains located in this zone. Africa's Mount Kenya lies just south of the equator, is 17,040 feet (5,194 m) high and has several glaciers on its upper regions. Mount Chimborazo near the equator in the Andes of Ecuador is also permanently snow-capped. It is therefore possible to freeze to death at or near the equator.

Quicksand drags you under

Quicksand does not pull the unwary victim down beneath its surface. Getting stuck in quicksand does not mean automatic death.

Quicksand, a mixture of sand and water, is about twice as buoyant as water, and one can take advantage of this buoyancy to get free. Of course, anyone who stumbles into quicksand, becomes hysterical and begins to thrash about wildly in an effort to escape will only work his body in deeper, and may indeed "sink up to his neck." However, the quicksand would not be pulling; the victim would be doing the pushing.

If caught in quicksand, experts advise, remain calm and free yourself by lying on your back, letting the buoyancy of the quicksand support you, and slowly rolling towards firm ground again.

Quicksand can ruin your day

Mount Everest is the highest mountain in the world

Yes and no. It all depends on how you measure height. Mount Everest in the Himalaya Mountains, rising 29,028 feet (8,848 m) above sea level, is considered the tallest mountain in the world. No other mountain rises so high above sea level. However, measuring height according to distance above sea level is only one way of doing it.

Another equally valid way is to measure height on the basis of distance from the center of the earth. If this method is used, Ecuador's Mount Chimborazo in the Andes Mountains, which rises "only" 20,577 feet (6,272 m) above sea level, is taller.

Mount Chimborazo happens to be about two degrees from the equator, while Mount Everest is far north of the equator. Since the earth is not perfectly round but bulges at the equator, Chimborazo by this measurement is nearly 2 miles (3.2 km) higher than Mount Everest.

The Himalaya Mountains are the greatest in the world

The greatest mountain range in the world is not even visible, for the most part. Undiscovered until this century, it lies under the Atlantic Ocean between the North American and European continents, and is called the Mid-Atlantic Ridge.

This gigantic underwater formation extends in a north-south direction from Iceland to near the Antarctic Circle, a distance of more than 10,000 miles (16,090 km). The Himalaya range, in comparison, is a mere 1,600 miles (2,574 km) long.

Because the water in this part of the Atlantic is so deep, most of these huge mountains lie far below the surface. The peaks of some of the larger mountains rise above the ocean, however, forming such islands as the Azores, Ascension, St. Paul and St. Helena.

The polar regions are very similar

Most people have only a vague idea of what the polar regions are like, and think the Arctic (northernmost) and the Antarctic (southernmost) regions are pretty much the same. However, there are a number of differences between the two.

The average temperature of the Antarctic at a given latitude is about 20°F (11°C) colder than the temperature at the same latitude in the Arctic. The Antarctic is by far the coldest region in the world, one reason being that it is a mountainous land mass. The Antarctic averages 14,000 feet (4,267 m) above sea level. The Arctic, by comparison, is for the most part at or near sea level.

As for summers, the temperature in the Antarctic seldom gets above freezing. The summers in the Arctic are brief but can get as hot as New York does.

Almost 95 per cent of the world's permanent ice is found in the Antarctic. The covering of ice and snow on the Antarctic land mass has an average thickness of 8,000 feet (2,438 m). The thickness of the ice pack around the North Pole, on the other hand, averages 9 to 10 feet (2.7 to 3 m) thick, although in some areas the ice may be as thick as 65 feet (19.8 m).

Life is far more abundant in the Arctic than in the Antarctic. In the Arctic are vast herds of caribou and reindeer, as well as the polar bear, seal, walrus, and many kinds of birds and insects. While plant life is not as varied as in more southerly regions, the Arctic does have 1,500 different kinds of plants. The Antarctic, by comparison, has little more than penguins, seals, whales, a few insect species, and some lichens and mosses.

Of course, the final proof that the Arctic is a more livable place than the Antarctic is the presence of human life there — Eskimos, Lapps and other peoples. Except for visiting explorers and scientists, no humans live or have ever lived in the Antarctic.

Summer in the Arctic

Metals, Minerals and Gems

Iron is the most abundant metal

Iron is not the most abundant metal on earth although it may seem to be because of its wide use throughout history. Aluminum is the most abundant, comprising 8 per cent of the earth's crust. It was isolated as a separate metal in 1827 and did not become widely available for general use until 1868, when an inexpensive process of mining and refining it on a large scale was developed.

Lead pencils contain lead

The modern lead pencil contains no lead at all. The writing part of the pencil is made of graphite, a soft, crystallized form of carbon, mixed with clay for hardness. The more clay, the harder the pencil.

Graphite has often been confused with lead — hence the name "lead pencil" — but it is a separate, unrelated substance.

A bug in amber

Amber is a mineral

Since ancient times, amber has been regarded as a gem of great value. However, it is not a mineral. Amber, which is yellow or brown in color, is the fossilized sap or resin of extinct evergreen trees that flourished millions of years ago.

The most interesting amber contains the fossils of prehistoric insects that were caught in the sticky sap as it dripped down the bark of pine trees millions of years ago. When the amber is transparent or nearly so, these insects are often beautifully preserved and can be studied in detail by scientists.

Tin cans are made of tin

The tin can is really a steel can with a tiny amount of tin added. Tin is far too expensive to be used to make tin cans, which are used once and thrown away. Instead, tin cans are made from sheets of rolled steel to which a very thin coat of tin has been applied.

Lead is the heaviest metal

Definitely not. Twelve other metals are heavier. They are: gold, iridium, mercury, osmium, palladium, platinum, rhodium, ruthenium, tantalum, thalium, tungsten, uranium.

The diamond is the most valuable gem

This isn't true. Carat for carat, the ruby is more valuable than the diamond.

Rubies beat diamonds

The diamond is valuable because it is so rare

The diamond is not a rare gem — uncommon, yes, but not rare. It is mined in many African countries, several other parts of the world, and also under the sea. The diamond, in fact, is the most common of all the gems, but is nevertheless an expensive, prized mineral for two reasons. First of all, it is beautiful. Second, it is costly to cut and polish because of its hardness.

The diamond is the toughest gem

Diamond is the hardest natural substance known but it is not particularly tough. The toughest gem known is jade, whose tightly interlaced fibers keep it intact despite repeated blows with a hammer. A diamond, on the other hand, is a single crystal which, if hit at the right point, will shatter.

Because of jade's interlocking structure, it can be carved into delicate shapes without risking fracture.

All gems are minerals

At least four gems are not minerals: pearl, coral, amber, and jet. Pearls are formed in oysters and other shellfish when these mollusks secrete a substance that hardens in layer upon layer around an irritating object (such as a grain of sand) that has become embedded in their soft tissues. Coral is the hard skeletons of small ocean creatures called polyps. Amber is the hardened remains of sap from prehistoric pine trees and other evergreens. Jet is a black form of lignite, a substance that resembles coal.

Pearls are found in edible oysters

An optimist has been defined as a man who goes into a restaurant without money and orders a meal of oysters, intending to pay for his meal with the pearl he expects to find. The poor soul will no doubt end up paying for his dinner by washing dishes!

Although it is possible to find a pearl occasionally in an edible North American oyster, these have no value as gems. Pearls of gem quality are found only in a rather small percentage of oysters that live in tropical waters, especially in the Persian Gulf area.

Pearls are not plentiful

The
Human Body

All people have the same number of bones

The normal adult human body has 206 bones, but infants have more bones than adults. The underdeveloped skull of a newborn baby has six gaps or "holes" in it, the largest located in the middle of the top of the head. By the age of two, the skull bones have grown sufficiently to close these "soft spots," and thus the number of bones in the skull is reduced. Also, the last five vertebrae at the lower end of a child's backbone gradually join to form a single bony structure, the sacrum.

In addition, the coccyx or tail bone, located below the sacrum at the very end of the backbone, consists of four tiny bones in some people, but five in others.

The funny bone is a sensitive bone

The so-called funny bone is not a bone at all. It is the ulnar nerve, which runs in a shallow groove close to the skin on the inside of the elbow. Pressing the ulnar nerve forces it against a nearby bone and causes a shock or a tingling sensation in the forearm and hand.

Tickling the funny bone

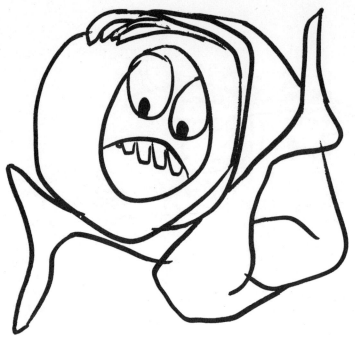

It's fun to be double-jointed

People who can perform feats of great physical dexterity are double-jointed

Acrobats and others whose joints seem to be made of rubber have the same number of joints as everyone else. They simply have more flexible ligaments than the rest of us.

A simple fracture is a broken bone with one break; a compound fracture has more than one break

"Simple" and "compound" are terms that do not refer to the number of broken places on a fractured bone.

A simple fracture is one in which the skin has not been broken by the shattered bone. A compound fracture, on the other hand, is one in which the broken bone has been knocked so far out of position that it pierces the overlying skin, bringing the bone in contact with the air and making an infection of the wound possible.

The heart is on the left side of the body

Because the aorta, the largest artery leading out of the heart, is on the left side of the body, it is easier to hear or to feel the beat of the heart on the left side, just to the left of the breastbone. This is not exactly the position of the heart, however. A small part of the heart is on the left side of the breastbone and a small portion is on the right side. The bulk of the heart is right in the middle of the chest, slightly tilted.

The pupil of the eye is a black spot

The pupil of the eye only appears to be black; actually it is a transparent hole in the middle of the iris. The pupil looks black because the retina, which lies behind it, is dark in color, and because the illumination inside the eye is small compared to the amount of light outside.

Cold, damp weather causes the common cold

Exposure to low temperatures by itself will not bring on a cold. The common cold is caused by viruses. No virus, no cold — no matter how cold and damp the weather. Arctic explorers have reported being free of colds during even the bitterest weather, and colds were almost unknown to Eskimos until the virus was introduced by outsiders.

However, many cold viruses flourish best at low temperatures, and this is why people come down with colds more often in winter than during the summer months. In addition, prolonged exposure to cold, damp weather, like fatigue, can lower one's resistance to cold viruses in the air.

Don't spread your cold!

history

Nero and his lyre

Nero fiddled while Rome burned

The Roman emperor Nero (37 A.D.-68 A.D.) is infamous as a cruel and evil ruler. He was also an amateur musician who took pride in his musical abilities. It is a widely held belief that this foul emperor played the fiddle while two-thirds of Rome was destroyed by a fire that raged for nine days in 64 A.D.

In fact, Nero could not have played the fiddle while Rome burned. The violin and similar instruments were not invented until the 16th century. If Nero played any instrument at all while Rome burned, it was probably the small harp-like instrument called a lyre.

Julius Caesar was a Roman emperor

Julius Caesar (100-44 B.C.) was a famous Roman general, statesman, orator and writer. He was consul five times and held the title of dictator, but he was never emperor. In Julius Caesar's time, Rome was a republic; the Roman Empire was not founded until 17 years after Caesar was murdered, when Augustus became the first Roman emperor.

Cleopatra was an Egyptian

Cleopatra (69-30 B.C.) may have been the Queen of Egypt, but she was not an Egyptian. She was part Macedonian, part Greek and part Iranian.

In Egyptian history, Cleopatra is really not very important. She was the last of the corrupt and greedy Ptolemaic rulers, and her importance lies mainly in her association with Julius Caesar and Mark Antony.

Pompeii was destroyed by molten lava

The common notion that Pompeii was destroyed by molten lava is wrong. It was not the lava but the fumes and ashes which killed many of Pompeii's inhabitants and buried the city.

Actually, there were two disasters which struck Pompeii. In 63 A.D., a great earthquake nearly destroyed it. The occupants of Pompeii began to rebuild the city, but during the rebuilding, in 79 A.D., Mount Vesuvius, a nearby volcano, erupted in a huge explosion. Pompeii and the nearby cities of Herculaneum and Stabiae were buried under ashes.

Had Pompeii been buried under molten lava, it could not have been so readily unearthed centuries later and so much of it so wonderfully preserved. Visiting Pompeii to see the remains of the city is now popular with tourists.

It is not known how many of Pompeii's 20,000 to 22,000 inhabitants perished during the eruption.

Santa Claus was not a real person

People who say that Santa Claus has no basis in fact are wrong. The beloved image of the fat, jolly, bearded man in a red suit who brings gifts at Christmastime is based on a person who really lived.

St. Nicholas, long considered the patron saint of children, merchants and sailors, was a 4th century Christian bishop in the Near East. He became the guardian saint of sailors in the 11th century and thereafter European seamen built many churches in his honor. It became the custom of choir boys of these churches to go around seeking small gifts on December 6th, the supposed birthday of the saint. The custom of giving gifts on St. Nicholas' Day spread throughout Europe, and eventually the celebration became associated with Christmas.

The early Dutch settlers brought with them to America the idea of the kindly, gift-giving St. Nicholas and the custom became popular among the colonists there. Thus St. Nicholas (or Santa Claus, as he was called) became the cherished symbol of Christmas in America as well.

St. Nick—patron saint of sailors

Two knights in armor

A medieval knight in armor was helpless

A persistent but mistaken belief about medieval life is that the fully dressed knight was a prisoner in his own armor. It is thought that the suit of armor was so heavy and rigid that the knight could not get on or off his horse without assistance, and could move his arms and legs only slightly.

The facts are otherwise. A suit of armor was well fitted and weighed only 50 to 55 pounds (22.7 kg to 24.9 kg), about as much as a fully equipped modern soldier's gear. A knight could move around easily, mount and dismount without help, climb ladders, and perform as readily as any other medieval soldier.

Ferdinand Magellan was the first to sail around the world

Many people are under the impression that Ferdinand Magellan (1480?-1521) was the first to circumnavigate the earth, but this is not true.

Magellan set sail from Spain on September 20, 1519. He crossed the Atlantic, reached South America and sailed southwards down the coast until he rounded the southern tip along a route now called the Strait of Magellan. He then crossed the Pacific and reached the Philippines where he was killed on the island of Mactan on April 27, 1521.

The voyage back to Spain was completed by the ship *Victoria* under the command of Juan Sebastian del Cano. Magellan, therefore, did not live to complete the circumnavigation of the world. The first commanding navigator to actually accomplish this feat was the English admiral Sir Francis Drake (1543-1596).

The Aztecs and Incas were largely destroyed by Spanish arms

The Spanish military campaigns brought considerable death and destruction to the Aztecs and Incas. However, far more damaging to these great civilizations were the diseases carried to the New World by the Spaniards. The Aztecs and Incas, having no immunity to the germs common in Spain, suffered epidemics of smallpox and, probably, measles and influenza. At one point, the natives were virtually eliminated from the coasts of Mexico, and the interior lost nearly 80 per cent of its population. In Peru, almost 90 per cent of the people in the area around present-day Lima died of foreign diseases in less than 50 years.

Flying vehicles were not used for military purposes until World War I

Since the first airplane was not flown until the early 1900's, it is commonly supposed that the use of airborne craft for military purposes did not begin until World War I (1914-1918). Actually, the first military air unit was formed in France in 1793, more than a century before World War I.

During the French revolutionary wars, the French government formed a scientific committee for the purpose of getting the best scientists of the day to contribute their knowledge to the war effort. Guyton de Morveau, a balloon enthusiast, suggested that the balloon be put to military use. The balloon, he argued, could be employed to direct armies in the field and to spy on enemy movements. Thus, the first airborne military vehicle was employed.

Military aviation in the United States began in the early years of the Civil War, when balloons were used by the Union forces for reconnaissance. When the war ended, this activity was discontinued, and the military use of aircraft was not revived until World War I, when heavier-than-air craft became commonplace. During World War II, military aviation was accepted for the first time as the equal of the other military services.

The guillotine and its uses

The guillotine was named after its inventor

The guillotine, a device for chopping off people's heads, was not invented by Dr. Joseph I. Guillotin (1738-1814), although it bears his name. Dr. Guillotin, a French physician, merely recommended that such a device be developed to kill criminals as swiftly and as painlessly as possible.

It was Dr. Antoine Louis who actually designed the guillotine. After the machine was tested using sheep and dead humans, France officially adopted the guillotine in 1792. It was at first known as the *louisette* after its inventor, but the name of the man who inspired its construction eventually prevailed, much to the chagrin of Dr. Guillotin.

The Battle of Waterloo was fought in Waterloo

One of the most decisive battles in history, the Battle of Waterloo, was fought on June 18, 1815, by Napoleon Bonaparte against other European armies. Napoleon received his final defeat in the battle. However, in spite of its name, the battle was not fought in Waterloo itself but in a village in Belgium 2 miles (3.2 km) to the south.

Charles Lindbergh flew the first transatlantic flight

The first person to fly non-stop across the Atlantic was not Charles A. Lindbergh. As a matter of fact, Lindbergh was the sixty-seventh person to make a non-stop flight across that ocean.

In June, 1919, long before Lindbergh's flight in 1927, John William Alcock and Arthur Whitten Brown flew from St. Johns, Newfoundland to Ireland in a two-engine Vickers airplane. Thirty-one persons flew non-stop across the Atlantic in the British dirigible R-34 in July 1919. (The R-34, in fact, flew back, making a round-trip crossing.) In October 1924, 33 men crossed the Atlantic aboard the German dirigible LX-216.

Lindbergh was merely the first to make a *solo* non-stop transatlantic flight.

The United States

Revolutionist vs. Tory

Most Americans supported the Revolutionary War

During the American Revolution, the Loyalists (or Tories) were a rather substantial portion of the population. These people thought the colonies should remain under British rule, and so opposition to the revolution was strong. No less a person than John Adams (1735-1826), the second U.S. President, estimated the Loyalists to be a third of the population, and believed another third were uncommitted to either side in the conflict.

The number of Loyalists varied from colony to colony, and from time to time. Many people simply sided with the army that was stationed nearest their community, or the one that appeared to be winning. As many as 100,000 Loyalists out of a total population of 2,500,000 left the colonies during the Revolution, primarily to settle in Canada. At one time during a period when George Washington had fewer than 10,000 men under his command, there were as many as 8,000 Loyalists serving with the British.

Contrary to popular belief, then, a large number of Americans, perhaps even a majority, disagreed completely or in part with the aims of the revolution, and remained loyal to England.

George Washington never served with the British

Because George Washington is identified as the father of his country and the leader of its army during the American Revolution, few people realize that he first served in the British army.

George Washington, in fact, served for nearly six years with the British during the French and Indian War, advancing to the rank of full colonel. He later put this military experience to use *against* England. Without this military background and training in leadership under the British, Washington might not have led the American Revolution to a successful conclusion.

Paul Revere made his famous ride alone

On the night of April 18, 1775, Paul Revere (1735-1818) set out on horseback to warn the people of the Massachusetts countryside that the British troops would be advancing the next morning. He hoped to reach Lexington and warn John Hancock and Samuel Adams, and then push on to Concord to rouse the other citizens.

On that famous night, not one but two men set out from Boston to warn the patriots. One was Paul Revere, the subject of Longfellow's famous poem; the other was William Dawes. Dawes went by way of Boston Neck and Revere by way of Charlestown. Revere arrived in Lexington about half an hour before Dawes. Hancock and Adams, being warned, fled. Then, before Revere and Dawes continued to Concord, a third man, Samuel Prescott, joined them.

Revere, however, was captured by a British patrol, and Dawes, though he escaped, had to turn back. Only Prescott was able to get past British lines and complete Paul Revere's midnight ride to Concord, which enabled the Minutemen there to assemble and to conceal most of the supplies before the British arrived.

While Paul Revere's role as a great American patriot should not be minimized, it should also be recognized that he had two other riders to help him on that memorable midnight ride.

The Battle of Bunker Hill was fought on Bunker Hill

The Battle of Bunker Hill was fought not on Bunker Hill, but on nearby Breed's Hill on June 17, 1775. This is why the monument commemorating the Battle of Bunker Hill is actually located on Breed's Hill.

Moreover, the Battle of Bennington, an important early victory of the American forces during the American Revolution, was not fought in Bennington, Vermont; it took place near Walloomsac, New York, 4 miles (6.4 km) northwest of Bennington, on August 16, 1777. The battle was so named because it happened after British troops were sent by General John Burgoyne to Bennington to seize desperately needed supplies stored there. Before they could reach Bennington, however, the 1,400 British and Hessian troops were met near Walloomsac and defeated by 2,600 untrained American militia under General John Stark.

Witches were burned in Salem

It is widely and mistakenly believed that people accused of being witches were burned in Salem, Massachusetts, in the late 17th century. Actually, the method of execution for those convicted of witchcraft in Salem was by hanging and, on at least one occasion, by pressing with heavy stones.

In Salem, 19 persons —13 women and 6 men — were hanged. While the witch hunt fever was one of the darker pages in American history, the situation was far worse in Europe, where thousands of persons believed to be witches were burned to death and beheaded during the fifteenth, sixteenth and seventeenth centuries.

"The Star-Spangled Banner" has always been the national anthem of the United States

Not so. *The Star-Spangled Banner* was written by Francis Scott Key (1779-1843) during the War of 1812 and thereafter was often played on patriotic occasions, but it did not become the official national anthem until almost 120 years later, on March 3, 1931, when the Congress of the United States passed the act which made the song the nation's anthem.

Furthermore, it is not widely known that Francis Scott Key wrote only the words of the song. Ironically, the tune of *The Star-Spangled Banner* was taken from *To Anacreon in Heaven*, an English song!

The Liberty Bell cracked when it was rung on July 8, 1776

The Liberty Bell in Independence Hall in Philadelphia was rung on July 8, 1776 to proclaim the Declaration of Independence, but it did not crack on this occasion.

It was on July 8, 1835 that the famous bell cracked during a funeral procession carrying the body of Chief Justice John Marshall through Philadelphia. The bell, after repair, was often used again, but in 1846, while being rung on the occasion of George Washington's birthday, it suddenly cracked again. This time the damage could not be repaired, and the bell was taken down and put on permanent display.

The day the Liberty Bell cracked

The first battle of ironclad ships was between the "Monitor" and the "Merrimack"

It is widely supposed that the first battle of armored ships, which took place on March 9, 1862, in Hampton Roads, Virginia, during the American Civil War, was fought between the *Monitor* (North) and the *Merrimack* (South). The battle actually involved the *Monitor* and the *Virginia*.

The North built the *Merrimack* as a United States Navy frigate in 1856, five years before the outbreak of the war. When the war began, the *Merrimack* was in the Norfolk (Virginia) Navy Yard in Confederate territory. To prevent the ship from falling into Confederate hands, it was sunk by retreating Union forces. Later, Confederate engineers raised the ship and converted it into an ironclad vessel. It was this salvaged, redesigned version of the *Merrimack*, renamed the *Virginia*, that fought with the *Monitor*.

The Spaniards sank the battleship "Maine"

An event that helped bring on the Spanish-American War was the sinking of the U.S.S. *Maine* in the harbor of Havana, Cuba, on the night of February 15, 1898. The explosion caused the death of 2 officers and 258 members of the crew.

When news of the sinking reached American shores, the Spaniards were immediately accused of sinking the battleship, and the nation was incited to outrage, particularly by conservative newspapers. "Remember the Maine!" became the war cry.

Actually, the cause of the sinking was never determined. It is still not known precisely what caused the explosion, or whether it came from inside or outside the ship.

As an excuse for going to war with Spain, the sinking of the *Maine* was a poor one.

The Pennsylvania Dutch originally migrated from Holland

The Pennsylvania Dutch — a community of religious people who live simply in eastern Pennsylvania — are not Dutch, but German. The sect has been misnamed perhaps because the German word *Deutsch*, meaning "German," was confused with "Dutch" by people unfamiliar with the German language.

The largest American city in area is Los Angeles

Los Angeles is famed for its spread-out geography and its many sections connected by what seem to be endless freeways. However, Los Angeles is only second in size; Jacksonville, Florida, far smaller in population, is the largest American city in physical size. Jacksonville has an area of 840 square miles (2,184 square km), while Los Angeles has a mere 464 square miles (1,206 square km).

Chicago is the windiest city in the United States

Chicago has a reputation for being a particularly windy place, and is well known as "the windy city." But is this

Chicago wind

reputation deserved? Surprisingly, Chicago ranks 16th on the list of windiest U.S. cities. According to the U.S. Weather Bureau, Boston (Massachusetts), Des Moines (Iowa), Omaha (Nebraska) and Dallas (Texas), to name but a few, are far windier.

Baseball was invented in the United States by Abner Doubleday

Baseball is regarded as the American national sport, and legend has it that Abner Doubleday created the game and its rules in 1839 in Cooperstown, New York. However, the term "baseball" was in use a full century before Doubleday is said to have coined it. Moreover, there is strong evidence that two English games, cricket and rounders, were the real ancestors of baseball. Rounders was introduced into the American colonies from England in the 18th century.

As for Doubleday's role in the creation of baseball, it is overshadowed by the contribution made by Alexander Cartwright. It was Cartwright, not Doubleday, who established many of the rules of modern baseball in 1845. He drew a diagram of a ball field with 90-foot (27.4-m) baselines, and had the batter stand at home plate rather than in a separate batter's box away from home plate. He made the infield diamond-shaped, reduced the number of bases from 5 to 4, and introduced flat bases instead of stakes. He also eliminated the rule permitting players to make an "out" by hitting a baserunner on the opposing team with the ball whenever he was not touching the base (a rule Abner Doubleday used in his games). While other rules he devised were different from those in present use,

Cartwright must be credited with creating most of the important features of modern baseball.

Cartwright also formed the first baseball club, the New York Knickerbockers, and his rules were used in the first recorded game on June 19, 1846, when the Knickerbockers played in Hoboken, New Jersey.

It is illegal to destroy United States coins

It is not illegal to destroy United States coins. Holes may be drilled into coins, and coins may be crafted or machined into jewelry or other items with perfect legality. Defacing or mutilating coins *and then passing them as currency* is what is illegal.

**Passing an
altered coin**

APPLES
25¢

food

The American English muffin

English muffins are English

English muffins are known only in America. What Americans call English muffins cannot be found in any English shops or bakeries.

Corned beef and cabbage is an Irish dish

Contrary to popular opinion, corned beef and cabbage is not commonly eaten in Ireland. It became a common food among the early Irish immigrants to the United States because corned beef at five cents a pound was all that many impoverished Irish families could afford at the time.

The Irish potato originated in Ireland

The common Irish or white potato, traditionally an important food in Ireland, did not originate there. It is native to the mountainous regions of South America, and today it can still be found growing wild in the uplands of Ecuador and Peru.

When the Spaniards first came to Peru, they found potatoes being cultivated by the South American Indians, who called them *pappas*. The Spaniards brought them back to Spain, where they were called *batates* or *patates*. From Spain, the potato gradually spread throughout much of Europe, reaching England and Ireland by the late 1500's.

While Europeans in general were somewhat reluctant to eat the potato, using it mainly to feed cattle and hogs, the Irish were enthusiastic and soon made it the most important item in their diet. In fact, when the potato crop failed in 1845, the Irish suffered a terrible famine.

French-fried potatoes are French

The Belgians, not the French, created French-fried potatoes. The Belgians call them *patates frites*, buy them at stands on the street, and carry them away in paper cones.

Chop suey is a Chinese dish

Although it is not certain who first made chop suey, it is thought to have originated in the mining camps in California. It was a sort of pot-luck dish made from whatever ingredients the cook, who was often Chinese, had available. Whether or not this is how the dish came about, chop suey is not known in China and is certainly not Chinese.

The Earl of Sandwich invented the sandwich

John Montagu, the fourth Earl of Sandwich (1718-1792), is credited with having invented the sandwich. Among the corrupt Earl's vices was an addiction to gambling. It is said that in order to avoid interrupting his card games for meals, he would order a servant to bring him a piece of meat between two slices of bread.

However, long before the Earl of Sandwich gave his name to this familiar food item, the ancient Romans were eating sandwiches of a sort and calling them by the name *offula*, meaning a bit or morsel. And since Roman times, a number of countries have featured sandwiches of one kind or another in their diets.

A snack for the Earl of Sandwich

Hauling spices in the old days

Spices were valued in the Middle Ages because they flavored and preserved food

As everyone knows, the search for a short route to the Far East and its spices led to the discovery and exploration of the New World. Spices, and pepper in particular, were terribly costly by the time they reached Europe because of the long haul over thousands of miles, across deserts, mountains and rivers. Nature took a terrible toll of caravans carrying spices, which were also often attacked by bands of robbers. Vast wealth and power awaited the discoverers of a new and better route to the East.

What is not commonly known is that spices were not used primarily to add flavor to and preserve food. They were sought in far-away lands and highly valued because of their use in the preparation of various medicines.

Bananas are picked green so they will not spoil in shipment

Many fruits are picked while still green to insure that they do not become too ripe during shipment and storage — but not bananas.

Bananas will not ripen properly if left on the banana plant. Even those intended to be eaten locally are picked green. If allowed to ripen on the plant, bananas lose some of their flavor, their skins sometimes break open and bacteria and insects enter.

The sardine is a species of fish

When you buy a can of sardines, you are not getting a particular kind of fish. There is no such creature as a sardine.

Sardine is the name given to several different species of herring when they are caught while young and small and packed in flat cans for human consumption. There is the European pilchard, a kind of herring whose partially grown offspring were the original sardines. There are also the New England sardine, another variety of young herring, and the California sardine, a young pilchard found in the Pacific Ocean. In England, it is the young of the Cornish pilchard. The Norwegian sardine is a fish called the sprat or bristling.

The sardine, in short, is any herring the canner chooses to call a sardine.

Chewing gum was invented in the United States

Chewing gum is not a recent innovation, nor was it first made in the United States. The ancient Greeks chewed gum from the mastic tree. The Indians of New England chewed a gum made of the resin of spruce trees, and in the early 1800's a commercial chewing gum was marketed in the United States using spruce gum.

Chicle, which was first used by the Mayans and other Central American cultures many centuries ago, was introduced into the United States about 1860 and became the basis of the first modern, popular chewing gum.

Ice cream originated in the United States

To many people, ice cream seems as American as apple pie. Although the United States does lead all other countries in the total amount of ice cream produced, ice cream is not an American creation.

Ice cream seems to have developed from flavored ice dishes that were eaten in ancient times. It is known that wines and fruit juices were added to snow in the court of the Roman emperor Nero in the first century A.D.

After the fall of Rome, ice cream disappeared from Europe and was not reintroduced until the 13th century, when Marco Polo, the great Venetian explorer, brought back from the Orient recipes for a more advanced dish containing milk as the main ingredient. The art of making ice cream then spread throughout Europe, and the early English settlers introduced ice cream into the New World in the 1600's.

Ice cream cools you off

Ice cream tastes good and feels cold, but it does not cool you, although you may imagine that it does after eating some on a hot day. Ice cream is so rich in fat and so full of calories that it ultimately makes the human body warmer, not cooler.

Mr. Priestley made a discovery

The soft drink is an American invention

The flavored carbonated water drink has been developed to a greater degree in the United States than in any other country, but it was more or less invented by Joseph Priestley (1733-1804) when the great English scientist made the first glass of carbonated water in 1767.

Some 40 years later, a Philadelphia druggist added fruit flavors to Priestley's fizzing water to make the first carbonated beverage. The drink was enormously popular and soon many competing products in all colors and flavors appeared.

odds and ends

Catgut rackets

Catgut comes from cats

Catgut, which is used in making stringed musical instruments, for surgical sutures, and for stringing tennis rackets, is not made from cats. It comes from the intestines of sheep.

Footballs are made of pigskin

Although the football is sometimes referred to as a pigskin, it is not made of pigskin. It is made of cowhide.

Iceland is a very cold country

Many people suppose that Iceland is a cold country because of its name and its location just south of the Arctic Circle. But Iceland is not a frozen, unpleasant land. The average January temperature in Reykjavik, the capital of Iceland, is about 30°F (-1.1°C). Thus, winters are not much colder in Reykjavik than in New York City or the cities of Western Europe, while summers are cooler and more comfortable.

How can a land so far north have such a moderate climate? Warm ocean currents called the Gulf Stream help to prevent extremely cold weather, and the many hot springs throughout Iceland keep the ground rather warm, even in winter.

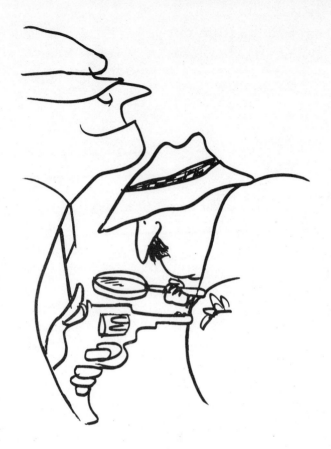

Search everywhere for fingerprints

Fingerprints are often found on guns

In detective stories the criminal is frequently caught after the police find his fingerprints on a gun. In fact, the police seldom find usable fingerprints on guns for three reasons:

(1) When a gun is fired, the force of the recoil moves the gun in the shooter's hand and thus smears the prints.

(2) Most guns are oiled frequently, and an oily surface will not make clear fingerprint impressions.

(3) People who shoot guns usually hold them so tightly that fingerprint details are blurred.

The bagpipe originated in Scotland

The bagpipe dates back to early civilization. It probably originated in the Middle East, perhaps in Persia, and was introduced to Europe and the British Isles by the Romans. This musical instrument is most popular in Scotland, but it exists in one form or another in Italy, France, Ireland, Germany, the Balkans and even Scandinavia.

Big Ben is a clock

Strictly speaking, Big Ben is neither the huge clock nor its 320-foot tower near the British House of Parliament in London. Big Ben is the bell in the tower that strikes the hour. It weighs 13 tons and was named after Sir Benjamin Hall, who was the commissioner of works when the bell was made in 1858.

index